D0470981

Discovering

WEASELS

Miranda MacQuitty

Illustrations by Wendy Meadway

The Bookwright Press
New York · 1989

Discovering Nature

Discovering Ants
Discovering Badgers
Discovering Bats
Discovering Bees and Wasps
Discovering Beetles
Discovering Birds of Prey
Discovering Bugs
Discovering Butterflies and Moths
Discovering Crabs and Lobsters
Discovering Crickets and Grasshoppers
Discovering Damselflies and Dragonflies
Discovering Deer
Discovering Ducks, Geese and Swans
Discovering Flies

Discovering Flowering Plants
Discovering Foxes
Discovering Freshwater Fish
Discovering Frogs and Toads
Discovering Fungi
Discovering Otters
Discovering Rabbits and Hares
Discovering Rats and Mice
Discovering Saltwater Fish
Discovering Sea Birds
Discovering Slugs and Snails
Discovering Snakes and Lizards
Discovering Spiders
Discovering Squirrels
Discovering Trees
Discovering Weasels
Discovering Worms

First published in the
United States in 1989 by
The Bookwright Press
387 Park Avenue South
New York, NY 10016

First published in 1989 by
Wayland (Publishers) Limited
61 Western Road, Hove
East Sussex BN3 1JD, England

© Copyright 1989 Wayland (Publishers) Limited

Typeset by DP Press Ltd., Sevenoaks, Kent
Printed in Italy by Sagdos S.p.A., Milan

Library of Congress Cataloguing-in-Publication Data

MacQuitty, Miranda.
   Discovering weasels / by Miranda MacQuitty.
     p. cm. — (Discovering nature)
   Bibliography: p.
   Includes index.
   Summary: An introduction to the physical characteristics,
habits, natural environment, and relationship to human
beings of the weasel.
   ISBN 0–531–18282–7
   1. Weasels — Juvenile literature. [1. Weasels.] I. Title. II.
Series.
QL737.C25M26   1989
599.74'447 — dc19   88–27033
                        CIP
                        AC

Cover *A common weasel out hunting in the undergrowth.*

Frontispiece *A group of young polecats cluster together in a nest.*

Contents

1
Introducing Weasels

The adult male stoat has a reddish-brown back, a creamy-white underside and a black-tipped tail.

Weasels Around the World

Most kinds of weasels have long bodies, short legs and furry tails. They are rather shy animals that are rarely seen. You may catch sight of an inquisitive little face peering out from the shelter of a hedge or a tail disappearing down a hole. They are alert and agile, and they can run very fast and quickly vanish.

There are many kinds of weasels including close relatives such as mink, polecats, martens and wolverines. Members of the weasel family are found in every continent except Antarctica and Australia. Some kinds of weasels are found in many parts of the world. The European common weasel lives not only in Europe but also in north Africa, Asia and New Zealand. The wolverine is found only in cold Arctic regions, such as Alaska, northern Canada and Norway.

Some weasels are known by several names. The stoat in Britain, for example, is a short-tailed weasel in the United States. Stoats in their white winter coats are also known as ermine.

Most weasels are wild animals that live in a wide variety of places: by the sea, in forests, on farmland and high

Wolverines have thick fur to keep them warm because they live in very cold climates.

up mountains. Some mink, however, are reared on farms for their fur. Ferrets are **domestic animals** that have been bred by people since ancient times to help catch rabbits.

What Do Weasels Look Like?

Weasels have long bodies, long thick necks, rounded ears and long sensitive whiskers. Each paw has five toes with long claws. But all kinds of weasels do not look exactly alike. Stoats and long-tailed weasels have a black tip to their tails, for example. Stoats and weasels are slender, while mink and polecats are stocky. Martens have longer legs than other weasels, and bushier tails. Wolverines have large bearlike paws.

The smallest weasel is the least weasel, which weighs less than 100 g (3½ oz) and measures less than 24 cm (9 in) from its head to the tip of its tail. A wolverine is not much bigger than a fox, but may weigh as much as 25 kg (55 lb). Its tail alone is about the length of a least weasel.

Male weasels are often larger than the females, sometimes weighing

The least weasel is the smallest kind of weasel. It measures less than 24 cm (9 in) from its nose to the tip of its tail.

twice as much.

Weasels that live in cold climates have thick coats to keep them warm. Common weasels, stoats and mink

molt twice a year, in spring and autumn, while pine martens molt in spring only. In northern parts of the world, where there is a lot of snow in winter, stoats, common weasels and long-tailed weasels shed their dark summer fur and grow white winter coats. This helps them blend in with their surroundings, and gives them protection from enemies and cover when hunting. Ferrets are often **albinos**. These animals have pale fur and red eyes.

The male common weasel is larger and stronger than the female.

How Do Weasels Move?

When bounding along, most weasels arch their long backs and bring their front paws and back paws together. The front paws land on the ground first and then the back paws are often placed in the same spot. This means that a weasel running on soft ground or snow usually leaves only one pair of prints each time it takes a bound.

Some weasels, stoats and mink run along with their backs straight and their bodies close to the ground. Polecats walk with their bodies and heads close to the ground, sniffing out the tracks made by other animals.

Small weasels, like the common weasel, are agile and can easily climb

The weasel can move very fast, arching its back as it bounds along.

Above *A long-tailed weasel sits up on its haunches to get a better view.*

bushy tails help them to balance when leaping from branch to branch.

Mink like the water and are good swimmers. They have small webs between their toes, which helps them to paddle through the water. They swim fast enough to catch fish underwater. Other kinds of weasels, such as the common weasel, also swim but usually hunt on land. Pine martens rarely swim.

Below *Pine martens climb trees easily, using their claws to dig into the trunk.*

over rocks, and run along hedges and walls. Every so often they stop and sit up on their **haunches** to get a better view before they rush off again.

Pine martens climb up trees, rather like squirrels, hugging the trunk as they go. They have long claws and fur on the soles of their paws, which helps them to keep a firm grip. Their

Weasels and Their Relatives

Skunks, badgers and otters belong to the same family as weasels. The weasel family is part of a larger group of animals called **carnivores**, which also includes the cat and the dog families.

Skunks live only in North and South America. Skunks and some badgers protect themselves from attack by spraying their enemies with a foul-smelling fluid from **stink**

Above *Sea otters eat all kinds of shellfish.*

Below *A Eurasian badger family forages for food in a wood at night.*

glands below their tails. This pale yellow fluid is called **musk**. It is easy to tell if an angry skunk is nearby because of the unpleasant smell that fills the air.

Otters spend much of their lives in water – streams, rivers and the ocean – where they find most of their food. The sea otters that live off the coast of California hardly ever leave the water. They eat **clams** while floating on their backs. They break open the shells by hitting them against a stone, which they balance on their fronts. When otters swim underwater they close their ears and noses to keep them from filling with water.

Most badgers are shy animals. Eurasian badgers live in groups underground in woodland. They come out mostly at night to find food. Earthworms are among their favorite meals. Badgers living near houses are sometimes fed by people.

A striped skunk holds its tail high to warn an enemy that it is about to spray its foul-smelling musk.

2
Where Do Weasels Live?

A long-tailed weasel peeps out from a rocky ledge.

Weasels Everywhere

Some kinds of weasels, such as the stoat and the common weasel, live in all sorts of places. Stoats can be found living near the ocean and way up on mountain-sides. They live in marshes and woods, on moors and farmland. Common weasels live in similar places but prefer areas where there are bushes and hedges in which they can hide. These weasels sometimes live close to people, perhaps on farms and even in towns.

Martens like to live among trees. They are good climbers, and they hunt for food in the treetops and on the ground. Most kinds of martens are able to live in forests of **conifers** and in woods where **broad-leaved trees** grow. In spite of their name, pine martens are not found just among pine trees but often live in broad-leaved woods.

Tayras live in tropical forests and can move very quickly among the treetops.

Pine martens live in remote forest areas or in rocky fields.

The sable is another kind of marten. Sables live in forests of conifers in cold places such as Siberia. House martens live in rocky areas as well as in forests and woodland. They also live close to houses.

Tayras are similar to martens but have shorter bodies and longer legs. They are found in South American forests. Sometimes tayras steal bananas from **plantations**.

Wolverines can be found in conifer forests. However, they also live in cold treeless places high up in the mountains and in the northern regions of the world.

Along the Water's Edge

Mink always live close to water. They hunt along the banks of streams and rivers, at the edges of lakes and along the seashore. They swim well and hunt for food underwater. There are two kinds of mink, the European mink and the American mink.

European mink are found mainly in eastern Europe. They are now quite rare, probably because so many have been killed for their fur, and because people have destroyed the places where they once lived.

An American mink hunts for food in the damp undergrowth.

American mink are more common and live all over North America, from the warm swamps in Florida to snow-covered Alaska. They are also found in parts of Europe where animals that have escaped from fur farms now live in the wild. American mink may have

Mink hunt along the edges of lakes and in the water. They swim well and dive to catch food.

driven their smaller relative, the European mink, away from some areas of Europe.

3
Staying Alive

A common weasel catches a harvest mouse and kills it swiftly with a bite in the back of its neck.

What Do Weasels Eat?

Weasels are hunters and eat small animals such as mice and rabbits. With their long thin bodies and short legs, weasels can easily chase their prey through the grass and into their holes or **burrows**. When these animals are scarce, stoats and other weasels will eat insects, earthworms, frogs, and even fruit and berries. The difference in size between male and female weasels may reduce the competition between them for food. The males, which are larger, are able to catch bigger animals than the females.

Polecats feed on all kinds of animals. The European polecat eats insects and animals as large as hares. Martens catch birds and squirrels as well as animals that live on the ground, such as mice. They also like to eat fruit, berries and any dead animal

they may come across during their hunting trips in the forests.

Mink eat whatever animals they can find. On land they often catch mice and rabbits. In the water they catch fish as well as crabs, **crayfish** and frogs. Water birds, such as ducks and gulls, are also a good source of

Pine martens catch and kill small animals, such as mice, with their sharp teeth. This pine marten has brought fresh food back to its tree nest.

food. In North America, mink eat muskrats, which are animals that are rather like small beavers.

When Food is Scarce

Weasels store food in hiding places for the days when food is scarce. Wolverines are well known for storing food. In winter they eat reindeer or **caribou**, which they either catch themselves or steal from a wolf or **lynx**. A wolverine could not eat a whole reindeer at once, so it takes off a part of a kill, then returns for more. Wolverines are known as **gluttons** because they seem so greedy.

The zorilla lives in dry regions of Africa. It likes to eat small animals.

Unlike most other kinds of weasels, black-footed ferrets eat mainly one kind of animal, the prairie dog. These are not dogs at all but **rodents** like rats, mice and squirrels. Prairie dogs live together in burrows on the North American grasslands.

Today black-footed ferrets are bred in captivity in the United States. This is because the prairie dogs were destroyed by cattle ranchers and

American black-footed ferrets are now very rare. Today they are bred in captivity and cannot survive in the wild.

farmers who treated them as pests. Without the prairie dogs, the black-footed ferrets died of starvation. Many ferrets also died from disease. Ferrets are now being bred so that one day they can be returned to the wild.

Hunting

A weasel captures an animal by leaping onto it and gripping it with its forepaws. It kills by biting the animal at the back of the neck. Weasels are unusual because a single weasel can kill an animal much larger than itself.

Wolverines also kill animals that are much larger than themselves. In winter they kill reindeer, especially those that are weak or ill. Wolverines can outrun these animals when the snow is soft. The reindeer's hoofs sink into the snow and slow it down, whereas the wolverine's big paws are

A short-tailed weasel carries off a pika it has killed. Pikas are relatives of rabbits and live in North America and Asia.

like snowshoes, enabling it to run over the surface of the snow. Once it is close to a reindeer, a wolverine leaps onto the reindeer's back and kills it by biting its neck.

The fisher is a kind of marten that lives in the United States. Fishers are among the few animals that kill and eat porcupines, which are well protected by a coat of **quills**. When a fisher finds a porcupine, it keeps well out of the way of its quills and only bites the porcupine's furry face. To defend itself, the porcupine lashes out with its prickly tail and tries to turn its quill-covered back toward its attacker. But the fisher moves around and around the porcupine, aiming more bites at its head. In the end, the porcupine is killed or stunned by these wounds. The fisher then carefully turns the porcupine onto its back to eat it. There are no sharp quills on the belly to harm the fisher.

Weasels hunt mainly by scent. They investigate every hole and crevice in search of their prey.

Enemies

Weasels, with their sharp teeth and claws, are often able to defend themselves against attack from other animals. Polecats can also turn their

A common weasel threatens its enemies by baring its daggerlike teeth.

backs on any attacker and drive it off with a nasty stench from their stink glands. The zorilla, or African polecat, pretends to be dead by lying still and letting itself go limp. If the zorilla is lucky, its attacker will lose interest and leave it alone.

From time to time, small weasels can be killed by cats, foxes and hunting birds, such as hawks and owls. Stoats may attack their smaller relative, the common weasel. Pine martens are at risk from attack by the magnificent golden eagle. Wolverines are sometimes attacked by wolf packs.

The main enemies of all kinds of weasels are people. Sometimes people kill weasels because they want to use their fur, or because weasels are pests that attack chickens or **gamebirds**. Often, people kill weasels accidentally. In the autumn, many unwary young weasels are destroyed on the roads.

The golden eagle is a fierce hunter and will use its sharp beak to tear apart any pine marten that it catches.

4
Family Life

A long-tailed weasel emerges from a burrow in Colorado.

A Weasel's Home

Most weasels live alone except for the time they spend together in the breeding season and when they are youngsters with their mother. A few kinds of weasels are more sociable, such as the tayras, which are frequently found in pairs.

If they can find enough food, weasels like to stay in one area. This is called a **territory**, or range. The large kinds of weasels, such as wolverines, roam over wider areas than small weasels. Male wolverines' ranges are from 600 to 1,000 square km (230–386 sq mi), while male common weasels' ranges cover only 10 to 250 square km (4–96 sq mi). Male weasels have bigger territories than females.

Where food is plentiful, weasels need only a small area to live in. In some places, mink that live along the seashore have smaller ranges than those living along riverbanks. This is because they can find lots of food in seashore pools.

Some weasels let other weasels know where they live by providing clues. They leave their droppings on bare rocks or along the paths they follow. These droppings smell strong because weasels mark them with musk from their stink glands.

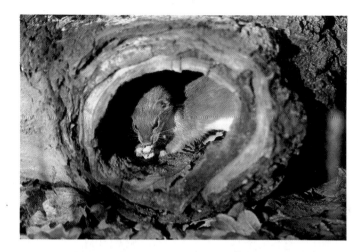

Below *Young short-tailed weasels run after their mother on the way to a new den.*

Above *A stoat hides in a hollow log to eat its food.*

A male and female European polecat begin their courtship.

Mating

Male and female weasels find each other in the breeding season. This is the time of year when they mate and produce their young. Males may mate with several females and sometimes they fight each other to win a female.

When the male wants to mate he grabs the female by the neck. She may let him mate immediately, but if not, he drags her about until she is ready. During the time they spend together, males and females often play and pretend to fight each other.

Some kinds of weasels, such as stoats, mate in early summer but do not produce young until the following spring. Although it takes only about one month for the babies to develop inside the mother, development does not start until many months after mating. Other weasels, such as the common weasel, mate in spring and

have their babies about a month later. This is because their babies start to develop immediately after mating. The adults can mate again, producing another **litter** in the same year.

Left *Male and female ferrets usually fight each other, but are brought together by breeders to mate.*

Below *Weasels spend a lot of time cleaning their fur, particularly after mating.*

Bringing up the Young

Weasels find a safe place called a den in which to have their babies. A den may be a hole in the ground or a bank, a crevice between some rocks, a hollow tree trunk or a burrow taken over from another animal. Pine martens may even use a bird's nest way up in the treetops for their den. Stoats and weasels sometimes make their dens more comfortable by lining them with fur from the animals they have caught and eaten.

Most kinds of weasels give birth to several babies at one time. Smaller weasels, such as the common weasel, have about five babies in a litter, but the larger wolverines usually have two or three babies.

At birth young weasels are blind and have very little fur or are totally naked. For their first month of life they feed on their mother's milk.

Above *Young pine martens have paler, woolier fur than their parents until their first winter molt.*

Below *A young stoat sleeps in a grass nest.*

Then their eyes open and they begin to feed on more solid food, which their mother brings to the den. Male stoats and long-tailed weasels help the mother to look after the babies.

When they are old enough, the young weasels go on outings with their mother, who keeps a careful eye on them to see they do not stray too far. She may take them to a new den close to a place where she can find food for them.

Young weasels learn how to hunt by playing with the animals caught by their mother. When they are about two months old, common weasels and stoats start to make their first kills. Soon they can fend for themselves. The family splits up and the young weasels go off to find a new area to live in.

Young stoats are fed on their mother's milk for about a month.

5
Weasels and People

Weasels are killed by gamekeepers because they attack gamebirds.

Weasels as Pests

Some people think weasels are pests. They are sometimes trapped because they kill gamebirds and steal their eggs. There are now few polecats left in Scotland and England because so many were trapped in the past by gamekeepers. Weasels can get into nest boxes that have been nailed onto trees for birds. They eat the birds' eggs or their young.

Mink can be pests, especially where they have escaped from fur farms. They snatch ducks from ponds and feast on fish taken from fish-farms. Like stoats and polecats, they occasionally get into hen houses and kill the hens.

Wolverines may be a nuisance in places where animals are trapped for their fur. Sometimes they destroy traps. They may also break into the trappers' cabins and steal their food.

Any food that they do not eat may be sprayed with their smelly musk.

Wolverines have been wiped out in some areas because they were trapped for fur or killed because they were pests. People now like to see them living in the wild. In parts of Colorado, wolverines imported from Canada have been released into the wild, in the hope that they will settle and breed there again.

Two wolverines are carried to their new home in the Rocky Mountains.

The Farmer's Friend

Farmers like weasels and stoats because they catch mice, rabbits and other small animals that eat the crops. Weasels often live in the farmyard and are small enough to wriggle through haystacks after mice. Pine martens are popular where trees are grown for lumber because they eat animals, such as squirrels and rabbits, that can damage young trees.

For centuries people have used ferrets to catch rabbits. The ferret is a

A farmer takes a ferret out of its box before putting it down a rabbit hole to chase the rabbits out.

kind of polecat and is trained by people as a rabbit catcher. Once a ferret is let loose in a burrow it quickly chases the rabbits. Nets are spread over the openings to the burrow so the rabbits are trapped as they dash out. Ferrets should be well fed before they are used to chase rabbits, otherwise they might kill the rabbits and stay down the burrow to eat them.

One hundred years ago, people thought ferrets, weasels and stoats were so good at catching rabbits that they took them all the way from Europe to New Zealand. Rabbits had been brought to New Zealand from Europe in the first place; however, in their new home they multiplied so quickly that they soon became pests, especially on sheep farms. Unfortunately, the ferrets, weasels and stoats did not manage to keep down the numbers of rabbits.

A rabbit is released from a net. It was driven into the trap by a ferret.

Ermine is sometimes used to decorate formal clothing, such as university gowns.

Furs for People

Weasels have thick, warm winter fur that is greatly valued by people. Some kinds of weasels, such as mink and sable, are better known as types of fur coats than as animals.

In cold northern areas like Alaska, Canada and Siberia, several kinds of weasels are trapped for their fur. In the past too many animals were caught, so weasels, such as Russian sables and American fishers, became rare. Trappers are now allowed to kill only a limited number each year.

American mink are trapped in the wild and reared on farms. Wild mink are normally dark brown, but there are a number of paler varieties that are bred on farms. These have rather glamorous sounding names like **topaz**, pearl and **platinum**.

Fur coats have always been a luxury although, nowadays, more and more

people prefer not to wear coats made from the skins of wild animals. Ermine, or the white winter coat of the stoat, has long been used for the

A stoat in its white winter coat.

robes of judges, lords, kings and queens, and for university gowns.

6
Learning More about Weasels

A long-tailed weasel hunts in a remote, rocky area of Canada.

Finding Weasels in the Wild

Most kinds of weasels are shy and hard to find in the wild. The best place to see them is in the country or in places where there is plenty of open space on the outskirts of towns. Even in these areas, few people see anything more of them than a small brown furry body rushing into the bushes, or a pair of bright eyes lit up by car headlights.

Some kinds of weasels, such as pine martens, are rare, and they are active mostly at night, so they are difficult to find. Stoats and common weasels are active during both the day and night. You may even see family groups playing together on sunny days in early summer.

Mink can be seen rushing along a riverbank among the stones and roots of trees, sometimes going in and out of the water, hunting for food.

If you have never seen a weasel of any kind, there are some signs that may help you find them. Look for the tracks made by their paws in soft ground or snow. Mink tracks can be found in sand or mud near the water's edge. Their marks are similar to, but wider than, the tracks made by otters. A field guide will help you identify them.

Another sign to look for is droppings. Some kinds of weasels, such as pine martens and mink, leave these on rocks and other places where they are easy to see. Watching birds may also help you find a pine marten. Some birds, like jays, will swoop down toward the animal to try to drive it away.

Keep your eyes open for paw prints and droppings when you are out in the country. You may see those of the common weasel, which are illustrated here.

fore print

hind print

droppings

Keeping Ferrets as Pets

Some people like to keep ferrets as pets. Once they are used to their owners they are friendly and playful animals. However, ferrets should always be handled carefully because they can bite and scratch. Most people keep ferrets in cages made of wood and strong wire mesh, which they cannot chew through to escape.

At one end of the cage there is a sleeping box filled with straw bedding. The rest of the cage is made of wire so the ferret can see out. The cage should be large enough for the ferret to run around. Some cages also have a wire mesh bottom so that the ferret's droppings fall through into a tray that is easy to clean.

Ferrets can be smelly animals, even when their cages are kept clean, because they have stink glands. Male ferrets are much smellier than

Ferrets are friendly animals when they are well cared for.

females, so are not such popular pets. If a ferret is frightened it will release musk from its stink glands, just as if it were being threatened by another animal in the wild.

Many people feed their ferrets canned or dry catfood, which gives them a balanced diet. Ferrets also like brown bread and milk, but should have some scraps of meat and eggs as well. They need to drink water, so a feeder bottle should be attached to the side of the cage. This is better than a bowl, which might be tipped over.

A ferret needs a roomy cage, but it should be let out regularly to run around in a larger enclosure.

Glossary

Albinos Animals that lack normal coloring or pigment so they have pale or white fur and pink eyes.

Broad-leaved trees Trees with soft green leaves that are shed in the autumn.

Burrow A hole in the ground that is dug by an animal to live and shelter in.

Caribou The name for reindeer that are found in North America.

Carnivores A group of animals that eat mainly meat.

Clams Shellfish with two matching shells.

Conifer trees Trees with hard green leaves that stay on the branches all year round. Many conifer trees have needle-shaped leaves and cones.

Crayfish A small kind of lobster that lives in fresh water.

Domestic animals Animals that are reared by humans and depend on them for their food.

Gamebirds Wild birds that are hunted for food or sport.

Glutton An animal that eats a lot.

Haunches The upper parts of the legs.

Litter A group of baby animals, born at the same time, from the same mother.

Lynx A wild cat with tufted ears and a short tail.

Molt To shed fur or feathers, etc. before getting a new growth.

Musk A strong-smelling fluid produced by an animal.

Plantation Land planted with one crop such as tea, cotton or bananas.

Platinum A precious silver-white metal.

Quills Sharp spines on the back of a porcupine.

Rodents A group of animals, including mice, rats, squirrels and beavers, that have large front teeth for gnawing.

Stink glands Parts of an animal's body that produce a foul-smelling substance called musk.

Territory The area that an animal or group of animals chooses as its own.

Topaz A precious gemstone, which is often yellow in color.

Finding Out More

The following books will tell you more about weasels.

Ivy, Bill. *Weasels.* Grolier, Ltd., 1985
Whitaker, John O. *The Audubon Society Field Guide to North American*

Mammals. Alfred A. Knopf, 1980.
Wild Animals of North America. The National Geographic Society, 1979

Picture acknowledgments

All photographs from Oxford Scientific Films by the following photographers: Richard Balharry 13 (bottom), 32 (top); Anthony Bannister 22; G.I. Bernard 20, 34, 36, 37; Galen Burrell 16, 24, 28, 29 (bottom), 33, 41; M.A. Chappell (Animals Animals) 14 (top); Michael Dick (Animals Animals) 10; Carol Farneti 17 (left); Breck P. Kent (Animals Animals) 32 (bottom); Richard Kolar (Animals Animals) 23; Michael Leach *cover*, 18, 26, 29 (top), 31 (bottom); Zig Leszczynski (Animals Animals) 17 (right); Ted Levin (Animals Animals) 32 (bottom); Miranda MacQuitty 42; Brian Milne (Animals Animals) 13 (top); Stan Osolinski 40; Press-tige Pictures *frontispiece*, 8, 25, 30; Robin Redfern 14 (bottom); Michael and Barbara Reed (Animals Animals) 31 (top); Leonard Lee Rue III (Animals Animals) 27; Wendy Shattil and Bob Rozinski 15; Marty Stouffer (Animals Animals) 21; Stouffer Enterprises (Animals Animals) 9, 25; Anna Walsh 38. The illustrations on pages 11, 12, 19, 41 and 43 are by Wendy Meadway.

Index